Productivity Mindset

------ ❧❦❧❦❧ ------

A practical guide how to multiply your productivity and time management for the overwhelmed

SuccessDailyRead.com

© **Copyright 2017 By Successdailyread**
All rights reserved.

This document is geared towards providing exact and reliable information in regards to the topic and issue covered. The publication is sold with the idea that the publisher is not required to render accounting, officially permitted, or otherwise, qualified services. If advice is necessary, legal or professional, a practiced individual in the profession should be ordered.

From a Declaration of Principles which was accepted and approved equally by a Committee of the American Bar Association and a Committee of Publishers and Associations.

In no way is it legal to reproduce, duplicate, or transmit any part of this document in either electronic means or in printed format. Recording of this publication is strictly prohibited and any storage of this document is not allowed unless with written permission from the publisher. All rights reserved.

The information provided herein is stated to be truthful and consistent, in that any liability, in terms of inattention or otherwise, by any usage or abuse of any policies, processes, or directions contained within is the solitary and utter responsibility of the recipient reader. Under no circumstances will any legal responsibility or blame be held against the publisher for any reparation, damages, or monetary loss due to the information herein, either directly or indirectly.

Respective authors own all copyrights not held by the publisher.

The information herein is offered for informational purposes solely, and is universal as so. The presentation of the information is without contract or any type of guarantee assurance.

The trademarks that are used are without any consent, and the publication of the trademark is without permission or backing by the trademark owner. All trademarks and brands within this book are for clarifying purposes only and are the owned by the owners themselves, not affiliated with this document.

About Us

One of the worst feeling in this world is being incredibly busy but not making any progress and certainly most of us have experienced this at some point of our life. In this challenging century, people need to constantly keep up and expand their knowledge and continually develop new skills to stay relevant and live a meaningful lifestyle. In every book written by our staff at **SuccessDailyRead.com**, we strive to bring you to reveal our key ideas and vast strategies to help you excel in every area of your personal and professional life. You will be given a ticket into the practice and of today's greatest achievers from successful businessmen, revolutionary entrepreneurs and outstanding leaders.

SuccessDailyRead.com is your go-to platform that help our readers to focus and succeed in their own arena. Our reader understands that today world had become more dynamic and the classic way of employer to employee relationship had evolved. No longer could our reader expect a corporate training to remain relevant in their professional field nor expect personal growth without reading and improving. All our readers are solely responsible for their very own growth and should be proactive to find motivation material to achieve their goal.

We believe while others dream of the future, **SuccessDailyRead.com** reader see it built. We believe our reader don't just create business only but they change the world in this revolutionary century. Regardless whether you're a student, a salaried worker, a home maker, an experienced entrepreneur or just starting your business, we hope that you'll never dare to dream and have the courage to make your dreams a reality.

You may be doing well in your life but certainly there's always room for growth and improvement. Our readers are not just here to fix their existing problem or remove any obstacles but they're here to create new possibilities, gain insights on today business challenge, improve their existing life and most importantly "short-cut" their learning curve by years so they can achieve their goals faster.

Bring your goals and take your life and business to the next level TODAY! Subscribe to our newsletter by visiting us at **www.SuccessDailyRead.com**

Let's master our ability to set good habits and positive mindset will have a lasting impact in our life. And we all have it in our power to get started!

Table of Contents

Introduction: Blueprint for productivity: It's all about taking baby steps 1

Chapter 1: The reason why people fail to be productive 5

Chapter 2: The Importance of time- Where most people spend, or waste their time 9

Chapter 3: The power of preparation 13

Chapter 4: Plan early and well 17

Chapter 5: Having a clear priorities & goals by adapting S.M.A.R.T goal setting 21

Chapter 6: Organizing priorities 27

Chapter 7: Setting realistic dateline 31

Chapter 8: Walking away from the negative ... 33

Chapter 9: Understanding the Pareto principle, 80/20 rule 37

Chapter 10: The good and bad kind of multitasking and avoiding distraction 41

Chapter 11: Power of meditation 45

Chapter 12: Speeding up the tempo 49

Chapter 13: Some things just aren't worth your time 53

Chapter 14: Speeding up decision 57

Chapter 15: Delegation, leveraging, outsourcing...61

Chapter 16: Use a to-do list..............................65

Chapter 17: Pit stops for top performers 69

Chapter 18: Resurrecting your dead time........73

Conclusion 77

Introduction:

Blueprint for productivity: It's all about taking baby steps

If you have purchased this book, then you are looking for something more than your average productivity book. You're sick of being told only practical productivity hacks that are great on the page, but just seem to fall flat in real life.

It is exhausting and the last thing you want to do is to expend more time on trying to implement things that you don't have a real motivation to do. I've been there. I've struggled to get up in the morning, and found my day slipping away from me. It's difficult and it can be very disheartening.

It took me a long time to fix what was wrong, and this is why I am taking a different approach.

Productivity Mindset

Practical tips are important, incredibly important. Without them, there is no framework for your productivity, but there is something even more important: Motivation.

You need to know why you are struggling to stay productive. You need to determine who you are not productive, why you want to be productive and what you can change in your mindset and your life. Changing your mindset and your outlook is more important than using the latest app to block your alerts. That will come later.

First and foremost, you need to focus on doing your best to clear your head, set your priorities and determine why you are working hard. In this book, we will go over a number of these aspects as well as ways to boost your productivity.

Part one of this book focuses on mindset. We will look at the reason why people fail to be productive, the importance of time and where most people spend, or waste their time, as well as the power of preparation.

Part two touches on something that I used to struggle with terribly: mastering your time. In this section, I talk about how to plan early and well, the importance of having clear priorities and goals by adapting S.M.A.R.T goal setting,

Introduction: Blueprint for productivity: It's all about taking baby steps

organizing your priorities and, of course, the art of setting realistic deadlines.

In the third part of this book, we will go over the topic of goals and how to focus on them. We start with the most important part- walking away from the negative. We then go over a vital aspect of time management and goal setting, the Pareto principle, 80/20 rule, the pros and cons of multitasking, as well as the power of meditation.

Part four is a personal favorite of mine, as we deal with increasing your energy and speeding up the tempo. We also touch on determining which things are just not worth your time, speeding up the decision-making process, and the benefits of using delegation, leveraging and outsourcing.

Finally, part four is a bit of a bonus section, where we focus on how to use a to do list effectively, taking effective breaks and making the most out of your time.

By the time we reach the end of the book, you'll have delved into the reasons behind your procrastination, and found your way into a more productive an energized mindset. Although this book is mostly focused on mental preparation, we do have some practical tips and questions to work through.

If you are looking to get the most out of your book, and reap the most benefits, then work through all of these exercises and tips as best as you can. Practical implementation can be a key aspect in making or breaking your success and your productivity.

So, without further ado, let's get right into it. I wish you the best of luck and I will see you in chapter one!

Chapter 1:

The reason why people fail to be productive

There are many reasons why people fail to be productive. These vary from person to person, but the main reason is consistent: mindset. Most people who try to be productive never take the time to think about why they want to be productive, or why they are expending so much energy and time on the task. This leaves them with a lack of motivation and inspiration.

Without proper motivation, these people never follow through with their plans for proper productivity. Simply put, mindset is everything. You need to know why you are going to do something, you need to have a clear idea of your future goals and you need to be motivated.

You also need to have a determined mindset. You need to have goals that are clear and realistic, and you need to have a plan to achieve them. Without these things, you will end up floundering. Trust me, I floundered for years before I realized that a clear plan and concise goals would help me immensely. It took a little bit of practice to implement this knowledge, but once I did, it was one of the best actions that I ever took.

It improved my motivation, my productivity and my over-all mindset. It was a great way to get myself going and I wouldn't trade it for the world. If you find yourself stuck on your mindset, then I have a few questions that you can ask yourself, which might help you clear things up.

- Why do you want to be productive? This isn't exactly an innovative question, but have a good, hard think about your motivation, what drives you and why you want to get the extra work done? This is important, as your motivation will keep you moving when you want to stop.

- What is holding you back? Are you scared of something? Do you find your plans falling through more often than not? Is your schedule chaotic? Think about what is holding you back and how you might be

Chapter 1: The reason why people fail to be productive

able to fix this (we will cover this in greater detail later, but jot down some notes for now).

- Are you willing to do whatever it takes? Being productive does take sacrifice, but the results are well and truly worth it. You might sacrifice the luxury of browsing Facebook in order to gain time with your family. It all depends on you and your personal problems, desires and lifestyle. If you want to continue, you need to acknowledge this now and make a commitment to yourself and to your work. Decide now to be willing to do what it takes, and you will benefit in the long run.

All up, this might seem like a lot of hard work, but having good and solid foundations is a good idea. Not only will it give you a good starting point, but it will help to keep you grounded when things start to get too much, or things seem difficult to work through. Keep firm in your belief and make sure that you have a clear idea of your motivations and determination.

Your mentality will shape your world, so really focus on it whenever possible. Check it with yourself and make sure that you are still on the right track wherever possible.

Productivity Mindset

Most people fail to be productive, and never manage to reach their goals, because they do not have the right mindset. Mindset is everything, so start it off right.

Chapter 2:

The Importance of time- Where most people spend, or waste their time

Most people are happy to spend their time multitasking and flicking from task to task. Most people are not, in fact, lazy. Often, when someone is struggling with productivity, it is assumed that they are lazy, or are unwilling to put in the work.

That couldn't be further from the truth. Most unproductive people are also very busy and hard working. It is usually just a problem in regards to where they are channeling their energy, and where they are using their time. This might mean that they flip from their task to emails and then to a phone call. This might mean that they spent two hours in meetings and were constantly working between projects instead of focusing on just one.

I know that I often used to feel very discouraged and tired, wondering why I was not able to get more done, concerned that I was just spinning my wheels and not getting anywhere. I worked hard, and I was always, always busy, and yet I always found myself late on the big projects and feeling like I was falling behind.

The lesson here is that you need to track and plan your time if you want to become productive. Start by tracking your work for a little while, making sure that you carefully note everything that you do. Do this for at least three days and determine where it is you actually spend your time.

Track your hours and your minutes and then make a note of where you need to make the change. This is a complete game-changer. No one wastes their time on purpose, so if you can do this then you will know where you need to focus your efforts.

People typically waste time on social media, emails, meetings, multitasking and over complicating home chores. More time is also wasted on dealing with things like clutter and a

Chapter 2: The Importance of time- Where most people spend, or waste their time

full schedule. Before you proceed, track your time and answer the following questions.

- Do you have any times during your day where you are not interrupted? Make a careful note of the times where you don't need to go out, or deal with children, or attend a meeting.

- Where does your free time go? Do you waste it away or do you have a set social life/ relaxation routine?

- What is your biggest time waster? Is it social media, is it emails, is it something else? Have a good look for patterns and decide on where your problems lie. This will help you later on and it is important to take a good, hard look at your schedule and where your time really does go.

Once you have taken a look at your schedule and answered these questions, you should have a pretty good idea of where your time is going and how you can get past it. Remember, most people don't waste time because they are lazy, but rather because they feel too busy! In the next chapter, we will talk about that and how you can get past it and become more efficient and productive.

Chapter 3:

The power of preparation

Preparation is such an amazing tool that I cannot rave about it enough. If you take the time to prepare, then everything runs so much smoother! In my job, I have to have a clear and concise outline for my day, as well as my individual projects. Without this, I can most certainly get things done, but I am nowhere near as productive as I need to be.

In fact, when I have a good outline, my productivity goes up by at least 30% or more, and it is a great way to clear my head too. Plans help in so many ways, which I will talk about in this chapter.

Scheduling

Having a good plan can be especially helpful in factoring in the plans for your day and deciding when you need to work. This is good, because it means that you can plan for how many hours you need to complete a project. If you have an open ended project, then it can drag on and you will feel like you are never getting it done. This can drain your motivation and leave you feeling utterly exhausted. A clear hourly work plan, and deadline, can do wonders for keeping you on track. Scheduling is a powerful tool that can be achieved through planning.

Preventing overwhelm

If you know that you have a huge deadline coming up, then chances are you will not take on a huge project or an extra community event. Plans help you from overwhelming yourself and crowding your schedule. It will also let you know when you can afford to take a bit of a break and free up your schedule a little. It is the best of both worlds and is a good reason for adding planning to your list of tasks.

Clear communication

Having a plan means that you can communicate it to the people around you. This might mean communicating your schedule to your partner, or making sure everyone on your team is on the same page for your work schedule. Either way, it

Chapter 3: The power of preparation

is a useful tool to have on hand and can prevent stress and arguments.

Less stress

If you have a plan, you won't be as stressed, and you will feel more motivated and everything will just flow so much smoother. If you have less stress, you will be able to think in a clearer way, stay more relaxed and perform better. You will also be able to enjoy your down time so much more, and after all, isn't that one of the major upsides to being more productive in the first place?

There are many other reasons to work preparation into your schedule, but these are some of the very best ones. I am personally a big fan of planning and I feel lost without it. Remember, the people who achieve the most, usually have a plan for the day, the week, the month and the year! They might not always stick to the plan, but having one is a fantastic way to stay productive, to move forward and to make sure that you achieve the goals that you set out to achieve.

Chapter 4:

Plan early and well

In the last chapter, we touched on the importance of planning and planning well. Just as a recap, in case you took a little break between chapters, we reviewed the following reasons for having a good and solid plan in place:

Scheduling: Having a good plan can be especially helpful in factoring in the plans for your day and deciding when you need to work. This is good, because it means that you can plan for how many hours you need to complete a project.

Preventing overwhelm: Plans help you from overwhelming yourself and crowding your schedule. It will also let you know when you can afford to take a bit of a break and free up your schedule a little.

Clear communication: Having a plan means that you can communicate it to the people around you.

Productivity Mindset

Less stress: If you have a plan, you won't be as stressed, you will feel more motivated and everything will just flow so much smoother. If you have less stress, you will be able to think in a clearer way, stay more relaxed and perform better.

So how can you plan and reap all of these benefits in an effective way? Well, it all starts with planning early and in advance. Having a clear plan of your day is fantastic, but if you make the plan at 12pm, it isn't going to be that effective.

A great way to do this is to start by planning your week and the tasks that you want to achieve. You can then look at your calendar, schedule in appointments and block out time to use for your work and projects.

Ideally, though, you should try and focus on planning your whole month. Of course, there is a good chance that everything will change, but try and block in some time for work and the existing appointments. This gives you a great base model to work off, and makes it so much easier to manage your tasks and your stressors.

So the moral of this is: Plan as early as you possibly can and you will reap the rewards. If

Chapter 4: Plan early and well

you can finish a task ahead of the deadline, then by all means do so. It will free up your time and leave you less stressed. Planning is a great tool and it is best that you try and get your head around it as quickly as possible, as it makes everything else fall into place better than any of the other tools in this book.

Planning related back to mindset, which we spoke about in the first chapter. If you have a good mindset, where you are determined and you have a plan, then you will have a much better idea of where you are going in your life and career.

Lastly, always take a moment to review your plan at the end of each day, as well as at the beginning of each day, to make sure that you are on track with your goals, your ideals and where you want to be. Sticking to these tasks is an excellent way to make sure that you stay productive.

Plan early and stay productive, calm and ready to tackle anything that comes your way. In the next chapter, we will touch in the specifics of goal planning and how you can create the best possible goals for yourself, so keep reading!

Chapter 5:

Having a clear priorities & goals by adapting S.M.A.R.T goal setting

If you have ever read an article about productivity, then you have probably heard about setting SMART goals. SMART goals come up in every aspect of productivity training, and they do so for a very, very good reason. SMART goals are fantastic for breaking down a task into an attainable action plan. By the time you have written a goal out using this method, you will have a very good idea of what you need to do, when you need to do it by, and how you will know when you have achieved it.

The acronym in SMART stands for the following: specific, measurable, attainable, realistic, time-based goals. But what does this all mean, and how can it help you and your goal setting plans?

Productivity Mindset

Specific-

You need to make sure that the goal you set is very specific. Instead of, for, example, saying that you just want to "improve your career", specify that you want to "get promoted into a managerial position within my current company". Having a goal that is specific, rather than vague, can do wonders for helping your harness your motivation and help you achieve the goal in clear and concise way. Be as specific as possible, in every case. If you want to lose weight and get healthy, specify every detail. If you want to achieve in your studies, specify a grade that you want to get, etc. The more specific, the better!

Measurable-

Making sure that your goal is measurable is the next part of this, but it is no less important to making sure that you achieve it. Make sure that you have a good idea of what you want to achieve and how that can be measured. Maybe you want to make a certain amount of money, or lose a certain amount of weight. No matter what you goal is, find a way to make it measurable. How will you know when you are finished? What is your goal and how could you show others than you had achieved it? Have a long think about

Chapter 5: Having a clear priorities & goals by adapting S.M.A.R.T goal setting

this, because a measurable goal is easier to achieve.

Achievable-

This is similar to the next point, but not quite. Make sure that your goal is something that is attainable. This means that you need to be sure that this is something you can do. Don't try and work for 25 hours every day, as that will never happen. Do not try to lose too much weight, since you have to account for your bones and muscle to some degree. Make sure that your goal is something that you can actually achieve. It is great to set big goals, but please make sure that they are achievable before you set them.

Realistic-

This is similar to achievable, but different in a few ways. This is about making sure that your goal is realistic. This means making sure that you have put a realistic time frame on your goal. Perhaps you want to finish a novel- a time frame of 1 hour isn't going to work, unless you have most of your draft already finished. Make sure that your goal is realistic. It is okay to dream big, but do not make your goals so unrealistic that you cannot achieve them and you get disheartened.

Productivity Mindset

Time-Based

Try and put a clear timeframe on your goal. This can be a day, a week, or a year. It doesn't matter, but it does matter that it is very clear and realistic. Keep this in mind and plan your goal accordingly. If your goal is open-ended, you can keep putting it off. If there is a deadline, you will be so much more likely to get it done and really work on it.

SMART goals are very powerful and it is widely recognized as being the best way to make your dreams come true in a realistic sense. If you find yourself struggling with productivity, then this can be a good way to get yourself started. It takes your abstract goals and desires and turns them into a very actionable plan. You know exactly what you want to achieve and when you want to achieve it by. It is clear, realistic and attainable.

This is a good way to increase your motivation too, as these goals no longer seem so out of reach and impossible to achieve. Instead, these goals are in your reach, if you just work smart and hard. This is comforting and I know that, personally, it helps me move forward.

No longer does my goal seem overwhelming. It is broken down, manageable and clear in ways that

Chapter 5: Having a clear priorities & goals by adapting S.M.A.R.T goal setting

I could never have imagined. If you are having trouble with your goals, give it a try and answer the following questions below:

- **Specific**: What is the exact goal I want to achieve? (Be detailed!)

- **Measurable**: How will I measure this goal? How do I know I have reached it?

- **Achievable**: Is this goal something that is reasonably attainable for me?

- **Realistic**: Have I given myself a good timeframe and do I have the tools I realistically need for this goal?

- **Time-Based**: What is my exact time frame? Is it a date, a time, or a point in the future? Be nice and specific/ clear about this.

Answer these questions for each and every goal that you have and you will find that things go much smoother in terms of achieving your goals and knowing exactly what you are truly aiming to achieve.

Chapter 6:

Organizing priorities

When people think of their priorities they usually think in one of two ways. Either they think of the broad and overreaching priorities, such as health, family, work, etc. Or they think about priorities in a smaller scale way, such as the approaching report deadline or a meeting. This is a common mistake and a very easy trap to fall into.

However, when trying to determine your priorities and where you should be focusing your time and your energy, you need to be considering both of these aspects. It is important to consider both the broad priorities, as well as the smaller, specific ones.

You cannot have one without the other and still have effective control of your time. You need to be aware of it all and you need to work this into your daily life whenever it is possible for you to do so.

Productivity Mindset

To start off, start thinking about things in a broader sense. What are your priorities in your life? Do you have a family that needs taking care of? Aging parents and a job? What about studies and your health? What motivates you to get up in the morning? What are the most important aspects of your life and how can you address these effectively?

Make a note of these, and then scale things down a bit. What about the tasks within these things? Do you have a big deadline at work, or a parent teacher meeting you can't miss? Are you committed to attending classes, or maybe you need to make sure that you attend the gym regularly?

This is different for every single person, but it is vital to make sure that you have a very, very clear list of your priorities, and what is most important to you. It is generally recommended to choose just three things, with one of them being health. This is a viable option, but if it doesn't work for you, then chose the three things you want to focus most on, and focus on other aspects of your life in a less intense sense.

Once you have this list, you need to make sure you put it into practice. If your priority is family, make time for them, for example. The same goes

Chapter 6: Organizing priorities

for everything else. Schedule down to the letter, and make sure that you have a very clear idea of the important deadlines and appointments within your over-all priorities.

Below, I go over the steps that you need to take in order to clearly evaluate your priorities and make them work for you:

1. Make sure that you write a list of all important deadlines, appointments and to-dos on your list. Keep these in line with your SMART goals and your values and try and be comprehensive.

2. List them from most important and the most time-sensitive, all the way down to the least important and the least time-sensitive. Schedule in your deadlines and decide when you are going to work on these projects.

3. Block this time and honor your commitment to yourself. Get to work when the time comes, and you will feel a lot less stressed and a lot less concerned about what the future holds. At this point, you will know your priorities, have clear goals and know what you are working

Productivity Mindset

> towards and I can tell you right now that that is a great feeling!

So next time you're feeling a bit stuck, have another think about your priorities, what the mean to you and where you stand with them- you'll come back to your work feeling a lot more focused.

Chapter 7:

Setting realistic dateline

When you are setting your goals and your priorities it can be easy to get caught up in the motivation and try and over extend yourself. Setting touch deadlines can feel good in the heat of the moment, but they only lead to more stress in the long-term, which is something that you want to try and avoid. It is important to consider the long term effects of your plan, and how realistic your deadlines are.

Have another look at the string of dates for your goals (often called a dateline), and pay close attention to the spacing. If you were to get sick, or an emergency was to come up, do you have any breathing room?

It might seem counterproductive, but factoring in for these problems is actually likely to boost your productivity, rather than deplete it. Remember, if you don't hit any of your deadlines, and you find yourself getting

Productivity Mindset

disheartened, you will most likely start to lack the motivation you need to be truly productive at a higher functioning level.

Temporary gains are no substitute for long-term, sustainable productivity. Pace yourself. It is always okay to push yourself a little bit, push yourself to do better and try harder, but never be so hard on yourself that you are doomed to fail. Accept your limits and work on pushing and stretching them gradually, instead of making everything impossibly hard and burning yourself out in the process.

I've been there. I have tried to take on studying and work and pushed myself to finish projects far faster than I should have. At the time, it worked, until I burnt out completely and had to stop working for a few months. I learnt an important lesson that day and now my productivity is consistently good instead of sporadically terrible or incredible.

Steady and even productivity is a great idea and it is very important to make sure you stick to this outlook. Trust me, it really helps things!

Chapter 8:

Walking away from the negative

Do you constantly find yourself surrounded by the negative? Do you find yourself being dragged down by negative comments and having to deal with people who clearly do not get it? Do you have to deal with work you hate and tasks you hate on a daily basis?

If you do, then you have my sympathy. It can be hard to be productive when you are surrounded by a lot of negativity, and harder still to find the motivation to change things. So how to do you do it? How do you stay productive with negativity in your life?

The answer is simple- you walk away. Now, this might sound insane to many people, but hear me out. Don't leave your job, but take a step back from the conversation with co-workers that is dragging you down. Don't stop hanging out with

Productivity Mindset

friends, but steer towards the ones who are uplifting rather than depressing. Try and focus on making a change, instead of giving into the status quo.

For example, is everyone complaining at the office lunch? Walk away from the negativity by bringing up something positive. Be persistent and things will eventually change. The biggest lesson to take away from this is how important it is to make sure that you don't internalize the negativity that is surrounding you.

Don't take the negativity on board and let it ruin your day. Instead, focus on the positive and stay uplifted. This is easier said than done as sometimes people seem that all they want to do is drag you down- but push through it.

Don't give into the drama and always focus on the positive. A very good exception to this rule is if you work with people who are going through hard things such as death and severe illness. Being overly optimistic can be a blow to them, to be sympathetic and, but then walk away and back to your desk when it is time to do so and try and distance yourself in that way. It is important to provide support to others, but don't forget to take care of yourself and keep yourself feeling healthy, happy and sane as much as possible!

Chapter 8: Walking away from the negative

After all, it is hard to be productive when you are feeling sad and depressed, but it is much easier if you are feeling uplifted and motivated. Read motivating books, listen to great music and do whatever you can to boost your mood and block out the negativity.

It doesn't do you any good, so walk away from it and enjoy the optimism and the peace. Your work, as well as your sanity and general well-being, will thank you for it!

Chapter 9:

Understanding the Pareto principle, 80/20 rule

While the Pareto principle started as a way to highlight the economic situation in Italy, it quickly developed into a fantastic business model based on productivity and other important aspects of business. The Pareto model is a very good tool and principle to keep in mind when you are working on something. It factors in a few things, and accounts for the division of work and the division of profits in a business.

This also applies to things like time. The principle states that 20% of your actions yield 80% of the rewards, while 80% of your actions only yield 20% of the rewards. Does this sound silly? Then let me explain. Say, for example, you were working on a project for a client, a big, important report. You might only spend two hours writing it, and 8 hours responding to emails, making calls, brainstorming, going to lunch and working on a side project. The big project is what will bring in the profit, but you didn't spend the most time on it.

This principle proves itself to be true over and over again, and it is difficult to refute. For example, 80% of the wealth in a country usually belongs to 20% of the population. It is a very applicable principle and has been used in business to streamline activities. So how can you use this to benefit you?

Simple. Figure out what your 20% is- figure out your core operations, your core tasks, the most important thing about your job. Figure this out and then focus on it. Streamline and outsource the other 80%, if you can, and really, really focus on the 20%. Give it your all and make it great.

If you cannot outsource the 80%, then at least leave it until last. Do the 20% first and do it very, very well, before you consider moving onto the rest of your work. This is a very simple way of looking at things, but it works so, so well. It allows you to focus on the work that is most important to you and it also allows you to reap the benefits of your hard work.

Chapter 9: Understanding the Pareto principle, 80/20 rule

It is all too easy to spend the whole day on the 80% and then never get to the 20%, leaving you feeling frustrated, behind and constantly struggling, despite the fact that you are working hard.

Remember what I said at the beginning of the book? Often, when someone is struggling with productivity, it is assumed that they are lazy, or are unwilling to put in the work. That couldn't be further from the truth. Most unproductive people are also very busy and hard working. It is usually just a problem in regards to where they are channeling their energy, and where they are using their time. This might mean that they flip from their task to emails and then to a phone call. This might mean that they spent two hours in meetings and were constantly working between projects instead of focusing on just one.

So instead of falling into this trap, make sure that you focus on your most important tasks, consistently. You should have a good idea of what they are from the earlier questions and chapters, so plug them into this principle and watch the magic happen!

Chapter 10:

The good and bad kind of multitasking and avoiding distraction

The good kind of multitasking

Is there ever a good type of multitasking? Multitasking is often talked about as being terrible for productivity, so can it ever be a good thing? As it turns out, yes, there are times where multitasking can be a major life saver and can actually improve your productivity.

The key is making sure that you choose the right times to use your multitasking, and that you know how to multitask effectively in order to save time instead of wasting it.

One such time is when you are commuting. If you travel by train, for example, then there is nothing wrong with using your time to read up on your latest reports or get some simpler work

Productivity Mindset

done. Okay, so this probably isn't the time for your most important work, but you might be able to knock some of the lighter work out before you even arrive at work.

If you have kids, you might find yourself having time to kill while they are awake and still need your attention regularly. This might mean taking the time to check emails while they are playing around you, or, if you have older children, you might be able to take a phone call while they are in the bath (if they are old enough for it to be a safe idea). Making the most of time that would otherwise be classified as dead-time is a fantastic way to use every second of your time to your advantage.

So before you write off multitasking completely, consider using it to your advantage. That said, there are times where you shouldn't multitask, which we will cover below.

The bad kind of multitasking

Unless you are utilizing otherwise dead time, then you should definitely not be multitasking. Using up time where you were already too busy to work, is okay, but introducing multiple tasks into the same window of time in any other situation is not a great idea.

Chapter 10: The good and bad kind of multitasking and avoiding distraction

If you are working on a big project, for example, then it is a good idea to shut off all other distractions and just focus on that project for a block of time. This allows you to really focus on your work and get things done in an effective, clear and concise manner which is very helpful when you are looking at productivity.

Anything that saps this productivity, especially multitasking, should be removed from the situation.

Tips to avoid distraction

Distraction is a part of life, but if you want to become productive, you need to learn the best ways to avoid it. There are many ways to avoid distraction, and I have included my favorite ones below.

1. Turn off your alerts. If your alerts are off, you won't be tempted to check Facebook every five minutes.

2. Do not check emails. Checking emails might feel productive, but it is a waste of your time and slows your productivity. Only check emails at certain times of the day.

Productivity Mindset

3. Schedule time for your projects and stick to it.

4. Limit meeting length and meetings wherever it is possible for you to do so.

5. Turn off your phone, aside from emergency contacts (such as the school, or your partner).

These simple tricks and tips can do wonders for eliminating distraction, but remember that mindset is everything. Stay determined and decide not to give into distraction and temptation while you are working on your project. If you can commit to this, then you are already half way there!

Chapter 11:

Power of meditation

Meditation has been used for centuries to calm the mind and bring focus and relaxation into the spirit. It is a powerful tool and it has recently been accepted by Psychology as a very valid technique for curbing stress and increasing productivity.

So how does meditation help reduce stress and increase how much and how well you can work?

Well, the power of meditation lies in taking the time out to breathe. If you are busy, it is likely that you do not get much time to just stretch and breathe and have a moment to yourself. It is probably very rare that your mind is quiet and this is what makes it so fantastic.

By introducing meditation into your schedule, you are giving your body and mind a chance to relax and to breathe, without having to focus on anything or worry about anything. Learning how to still your mind, focus on your breathing and center yourself is amazing for productivity. You'll feel calmer once you are finished, less stressed and more focused and this does wonders for getting things done.

By lowering your heartrate and slowing your breathing, you are effectively letting your body know that there is no threat and that it can relax. This is a great tool for centering yourself, especially if you learn to use it to your advantage.

How to meditate?

Meditation is simple once you get the hang of it. Most people feel that it is complicated and that they have to devote hours and hours to it, but that couldn't be further from the truth. Meditation, in its simplest form, is teaching yourself to slow down.

Meditation is all about slowing things down, focusing in aspects of your body like your breathing and the feeling of the ground beneath you. You could focus on taking in deep, slow breaths, and try not to think of anything else. You can spend five minutes grounding yourself and finding peace in a busy day, or you could set aside a whole hour to really work on clearing your mind and energizing your body. The great thing about meditation is that you can tailor it to

Chapter 11: Power of meditation

your needs and to what most and best suits your lifestyle.

5 Minute meditation

If you only have five minutes in a very busy day, but you feel unfocused, stressed and overwhelmed.

1. Start by sitting (not lying) in a comfortable position. Shut your eyes and take a deep breath.

2. Try taking a few, deep breaths and then let them flow naturally. Focus on the rhythm of your breathing and try not to think of anything else. Just breathe.

3. If your mind wonders, do not get angry at yourself, just gently bring it back to your breathing and keep going.

4. Feel the tension leave your body and just breathe, letting everything else fade away.

5. Finish and stretch, feeling refreshed and ready to go on with your work.

This is a great technique if you work in an office and feel tired and overwhelmed. If you need an extra little pick me up, plug into a YouTube video about meditation and take a 5 minutes guided meditation instead- they will provide all the necessary instructions. Still, if you can't access anything, then this quick little meditation provided above is wonderfully portable!

Chapter 12:

Speeding up the tempo

So now you have a good idea about how to plan your goals, refocus your efforts and plan your day so that you are getting the most done that you possibly can. But what if it still feels like too much, and you feel too exhausted to actually do everything that you wanted?

If that sounds like you then don't worry, you are most definitely not alone. Most people feel like this at some point of their lives, so you are in good company. That said, it can feel terrible while you are experiencing it and it takes some focus to pull yourself out of the funk.

The first thing to work on is speeding up the pace, by increasing your energy. There are many ways that you can go about improving your energy, and I've compiled a list of my favorite ones below. Use the ones that work for you, and discard the rest. After all, you know yourself best!

Tips for increasing your energy

1. Get enough sleep. This might sound counterproductive, but getting enough sleep is a great way to make sure you have enough energy to work through the day.

2. Have good food on hand. Don't just stuff your body full of junk food, instead, focus on more wholesome foods with sustainable energy, like wholegrains and protein.

3. Keep clutter to a minimum. Clutter is probably more draining than you realize. Take the time to clean out your office, desk and room. You'll feel more refreshed, more energized and far more ready to go.

4. Keep the room at optimal temperature. You don't want to make things too hot or too cold. Keep things at a comfortable temperature and your energy will increase, especially while you are working.

5. Exercise. Regular exercise is great for your body and your heart and boosts your

Chapter 12: Speeding up the tempo

overall health and energy in a big, big way.

6. Keep your goals in mind! This isn't all physical and mindset is key, do make sure that you keep your goals and your reasons in mind every time you start to get exhausted. Write them down and stick them up if you have to, and power through it. Remember why you are doing this and remember that you are capable!

These tips should help you stay on top of your energy and leave you feeling pretty great. If they don't and the problem persists then it is always a good idea to have a quick check in with your doctor, just to make sure that you are doing okay. Your health is important, so do whatever you need to do in order to take care of it!

Your job can wait, but your body can't, so put your mental and physical wellbeing first and natural productivity will follow in big way.

Chapter 13:

Some things just aren't worth your time

If your energy is low, you feel like you are running on fumes and you are still running around doing it all, then you might need to reconsider what you are doing. This involves taking a good, hard look at yourself and determining whether or not an activity or task is really worth your time.

This can be a tough call to make, in all areas of your life, and you need to think this one through when you are feeling a little less exhausted. So, if you are feeling burnt out, go and take a power nap of twenty minutes or so, before you attempt these questions. If that is not an option, have a big drink of cold water, go for a five minute walk and then come back. You need to be refreshed for this one.

Productivity Mindset

How do you know if something is not worth your time?

So, now that you are refreshed and ready to go, we'll be tackling this topic, and it is most certainly a tricky one. How do you know if something is not worth your time?

Well, start by thinking about the things that drain you, the things that leave you feeling exhausted and tired, and uninspired. What about the things that you have said yes to, just because you feel like you have no other choice? What about the things that you just blatantly hate?

1. Start by writing a list of all of these things, from the uninspiring, up until the most hated items on your list.

2. Next, make a note of their importance. You might hate accounting, but it is vital to your business and work, so it is important to keep on top of that.

3. Have a good, hard look at the list. If you hate something, but it is vital, then make plans to outsource it. If you hate it, but it is not vital, then drop it. If you are not inspired by it, and it is not important, then drop it or scale back on it.

Chapter 13: Some things just aren't worth your time

This can be hard at first. We are programmed to take more on and to make sure that we always please everyone, but this is a destructive habit. If you hate what you do, and you want to make a positive and meaningful change in your life, then this is a good place to start.

Be as ruthless as you need to and cull anything that doesn't bring you enjoyment, or benefit your life. Cull it all until you are only left with things that are important, things that make you happy and things that you have to do for the sake of your wellbeing.

Anything else isn't worthy of your time. Anything else should be dumped, outsourced or reduced. If you have a commitment, honor it, but get out as soon as you can. If there is no commitment, drop it as soon as possible.

By doing this you are freeing up mental energy to succeed, but you are also freeing up physical energy as well as your time. You can use this time and energy to invest in something that you love and that you enjoy, or you can use this energy to further your productivity and to work harder.

It is up to you, but I guarantee that you will feel so much better for it. It can be hard to cut back

Productivity Mindset

at first, but it is so worth it in the end. Manage what you need to do, and what you enjoy and just let the rest go, because it is just not worth your time, and it never was to begin with.

Once you start, you'll never look back.

Chapter 14:

Speeding up decision

If you have ever found yourself faced with a huge decision, then you know how hard it can be to make it, and to wade through all of your different options and possible strategies. It can be confusing and it can be overwhelming. This is especially true if it is a big business decision and you are concerned about the outcome in terms of your job of what you need to accomplish in life.

So what can you do about it? Well, the first step is to take a deep breath and re-focus on the task at hand. Ideally, you want to be able to make the decision as quickly as possible (to keep productivity and momentum), but you also want to make the best choice for you and your career.

If you find yourself overwhelmed with a big decision, then there are a few steps that you can follow, consistently, that will help you beat overwhelm, work through the facts, and move forward again.

Reducing analysis paralysis in 10 steps

1. Analysis paralysis is the term for getting overwhelmed with a decision. If you want to beat it, start by taking a few conscious moments to really think about the decision and what it means for you.

2. If you have the time, jot down the pros and cons of the decision and go through them carefully.

3. Consider your values, your overreaching goals and your current workload. Keep all of this in your head for the next step- even jot it down if you like.

4. Have a look at the pros, cons and decision and see if it aligns with your goals and values. If not, consider not doing it/ or choosing the lesser of two evils route.

5. If it lines up, then you will need to consider if the pros and cons are worth it. Do the pros outweigh the cons or is it the other way around.

Chapter 14: Speeding up decision

6. Consider if there are any major, damaging effects, like a loss of your health and wellbeing, or a likelihood that you will affect your family in a negative way. If so, consider carefully if they are worth it.

7. Consider your other commitments and how it related to things. Will such decisions affect the rest of your tasks and commitments in a negative, positive or neutral light?

8. Look at your gut feeling and your intuition. If every part of you is screaming to not do it and you just do not want to make that decision, then step back. If you really want to go for it, don't force yourself to stop, and vice versa. So long as you see no major problems in doing so, listen to your intuition- often, it is right.

9. Make the decision and inform the relevant parties. Don't stress or stew about it. If you need to get approval from someone else first, do so, but try not to let other people sway your decision too much, unless they bring up a huge point that you did not think of (although that is unlikely).

Productivity Mindset

10. Don't back out. Stick to your decision unless you discover that there are major issues in doing so. For the most part, that should not be the case, and you will discover that regardless of your decision, things are going to be okay. Keep in mind that this is not the end of the world, so stick to your decision and move on.

These steps are here for you to use if you have a few minutes to make a decision. If you have less than that, just take a deep breath, think it through and then go with your knowledge and intuition. In all cases, it is important that you learn to trust yourself! You know what you are doing- you are good at what you are doing and you are making an informed and rational choice.

So take a deep breath and let go of the stress. You're making great choices and you have gotten this far, so trust yourself and your instincts.

Chapter 15:

Delegation, leveraging, outsourcing

When it comes to freeing up your time and focusing on what is really important, there are three words that you really need to learn and remember. These words are delegation, leveraging and outsourcing. If you can master these three concepts and the different connotations behind each one, then you are very likely to find a lot of success for yourself in the future.

You are likely to free up your time, ease your stress and be able to focus on that key, core 20% of work that is so important to your profits and your goals.

Delegation

Delegation is the process of scaling back on your workload and letting someone else handle it, usually an existing contact or friend. For example, if you are under a big workload, you might delegate doing the dishes to your partner. If you are working with a client, you might delegate phone calls to an assistant, and so forth. Delegation is all about striking the balance within your current organization, and can be a great way to help level the playing field a little.

Leveraging

Leveraging is the concept of taking your existing assets, and using them to gain better assets that further the business. For example, you can leverage your business by taking out a loan, which you use to further your business investments and you will, hopefully, see returns on it. Leverage is very powerful and it allows you to use what you already have to get what you need. You can leverage money, or your time and hard work.

Outsourcing

Outsourcing is similar to delegation, but different in a few core ways. You are still offloading the work, but instead of using someone that you are already in contact with, you find another, skilled person (often outside of the organization), to handle your current problem. This can mean that you hire a cleaner

Chapter 15: Delegation, leveraging, outsourcing

to do your dishes, or hire an accountant to do your taxes, instead of struggling with them yourself. Outsourcing is powerful as you are getting someone who is stilled at what they do to handle the task that you are not skilled at, or that you do not have time for.

How to know when to do it?

So now that you know the difference between the terms and how they can benefit you and your business (or your home life and personal workload!) the question turns to how do you know when to outsource? Is there some criteria to use? And how do you know when you have made the right choice? After all, delegating, leveraging and outsourcing can be very daunting.

When it comes to delegating and outsourcing then the criteria become quite clear. If it is not part of your 20%, then you can probably outsource it! If you really need to get your bookkeeping in order, but it takes you hours each day, then hiring a professional will cut down on time and make sure that it gets done right. If you want to send out marketing material, but it is just not your strong suite, then you are probably better off not doing it yourself.

Productivity Mindset

Consider how much time you have to work on tasks and if you have enough of it. Consider your own health and how much time off you are getting. Then consider if you have the money to fund outsourcing. Delegation might work for the short-term, but eventually your partner will get upset at all those dishes! So try and plan in advance, and use delegation when necessary, and outsourcing for long-term needs and services.

In terms of leveraging, this might take more thought. If you are leveraging your business, make sure that you have a solid base of research to back you up and make things work. If you are leveraging your time, make sure you use it as wisely as you can, and that you are sure of your success. Leveraging is a powerful tool, so use it wisely!

Eventually, you will learn to know when delegation is or isn't going to work for you. Once you have mastered it, you are already half way to productivity victory.

Chapter 16:

Use a to-do list

Using a to do list might be the simplest hack in this book, but I still swear by it to this day. Having a clear, and concise list of things that you need to do is a great way to kick yourself into high gear and get back to work. It gives you great boundaries, deadlines and everything else that is usually needed to fuel someone into success!

How can it help you get things done?

A to do list is a great tool when it comes to boosting your productivity. One of the reasons for this is the fact that it makes it easy to know what you need to do next. This means that there is no time wasted floundering and wondering what you should be doing and working through.

You know what your next task is and you know how busy you are that day. Some days you might have only one thing on your to do list, but other days might see you juggling ten things (although

Productivity Mindset

this is not recommended for optimum productivity).

It is also helpful in clearing your head and making you feel less stressed about it all. Having a million projects running around your head can be draining, to say the least! It is important to dump all of that information onto a page (or word document) from time to time.

Personally, I recommend using a paper and pen list, because I find that you switch processes, slow down and become more creative and more settled when you do that. If it is out of your reach, or just doesn't appeal to you then feel free to use technology.

They key thing here is putting your thoughts and ideas down, working through them and deciding on what you should do and focus on next.

Once you have mastered this, you will find that you are less stressed, more focused and your ideas are so much clearer. It's a little thing and it is sort of old fashioned, but it is a game changer, so if you don't make regular lists, start doing them!

Write them the night before, or the morning before work. Write them before you start, or

Chapter 16: Use a to-do list

when you are feeling overwhelmed. They help and I hope that you find that out for yourself.

How to write a great to do list

It seems silly to include instructions for this, but writing a good to do list is sort of an art form. To start with, just jot down everything that you need to do. Even if that means you write down that you need to cook dinner. Write it all down, in no particular order. Keep writing until it is all there.

Then pull it all apart and start working through it. Put home chores in one pile (list), and put work things in another. Then go further and narrow down personal commitments, deadlines and other important parts of your list.

What do you need to do today? If possible, block tasks off into similar groups (emails with emails, for example), and chunk it that way. Cross out the non-essentials and don't put too much pressure on yourself to get it all done.

Choose your top five items that you absolutely have to do. If one of them is an appointment, then don't focus on it until it is time. For the rest, block out some time in your day and get to it as quickly as possible.

Productivity Mindset

By writing it all down, and working through it, you can be sure that you are not forgetting anything important. This will take a huge weight off your shoulders (trust me!), and it will make it so much easier to get through your tasks without constantly worrying and stressing about what else you need to do, should do, or should be focusing your time on.

Write a to-do list, clear your head and get started!

Chapter 17:

Pit stops for top performers

It is a common misconception that top performers do not need breaks and that they just keep working in a super human way, but that could not be further from the truth. One key mindset difference that sets top performers apart from everyone else, is that they know very well the importance of taking breaks and taking great care of themselves.

They take care of their bodies, minds and souls and they make sure that they get what they need to improve their productivity and keep going! In this chapter, I will be going over the best ways to give yourself a boost during work and a few great break ideas (so that you come back feeling refreshed and recharged!).

Productivity Mindset

How to tune up and keep going

If you find yourself getting a little tired and struggling to focus then it might be time for a little refresher. In this I mean that you should spend some time taking care of yourself. This can come in many ways, but the key is to keep it brief, disconnect from work for a moment, and then move forward.

1. If you work at home, take a shower! This is a good way to wake yourself up. Don't make the shower too warm, and use it as a little refresher to soothe tired muscles, to stand and stretch and to make sure that you stay awake and alert. If you work at an office, try splashing cold water on your face, washing your hands and freshening up a little instead.

2. Eat something decent. Don't grab a coffee or a candy bar. Instead, go for some nuts and water, or a piece of fruit. This is a good way to make sure that you keep your energy levels up, stave off hunger and get through it all without driving yourself insane. Good food helps your brain and body function better, so you'll be doing yourself a favor.

Chapter 17: Pit stops for top performers

3. Stay hydrated! We touched on this in the point above, but never underestimate how important it is for you to stay hydrated through the day. If you feel sluggish and tired or a headache is just around the corner, consider getting up and grabbing some water. I guarantee that it will help and it certainly won't hurt!

4. Meditate. Earlier in the book, I wrote a whole chapter on meditation, so I clearly think that it is important. I stick by that and I want to add that meditation is a fantastic way to feel better at the office, when you cannot leave your desk. It is quick, easy and you'll be more focused for it.

5. Uplifting music. Sometimes, a good healthy dose of uplifting music is all that you need to get yourself on track again. Play your favorite tunes- just remember to use headphones if you have other people around you.

So next time you are feeling a little bit sluggish, try these tips and see what they can do for you.

Productivity Mindset

10 Best Break ideas!

If you have a scheduled break, then try and get away from your computer wherever possible. If that is not possible, then we have included a few options for you too! From park walks to office lunches, here are our best ideas for having a great and refreshing break!

1. Take a walk in the park
2. Get a haircut or sneaky massage
3. Have a wholesome lunch
4. Read a book
5. Listen to some music
6. Go out for coffee and savor it
7. Call a loved one
8. Read someone uplifting online
9. Pray or meditate
10. Work on a hobby or pet project

Chapter 18:

Resurrecting your dead time

Where is your time going?

The first step to determining where your time is going, is to track it. You will have done this in the first part of the book, so at this point it is important to have a look at those notes. If you have not done it yet, then now is the time. Doing so is very helpful and will give you a good idea of your biggest time wasters.

Once you have had a good look at that, determine where your dead time is. Do you commute? Make dinner? Wash dishes or spend a lot of time in meetings? Determine where you spend most of your dead time and start making plans to reclaim it!

This process is fairly simple but, like with most things. It starts with a keen awareness of the situation, which makes it easier to get your head around and work with what you have. So track, track, track and then examine for any patterns.

Once you have done that, move on to the second half of the chapter!

How can you reclaim your time?

Reclaiming your time is a process and it starts by determining where your dead time is and how you can work this in to your productivity.

We mentioned this in our chapter about multitasking, but it is such a valid point that we had to clarify it again. Reclaiming your dead time is easy if you know what you are looking for, and how to use it.

One such time, when you have dead time that you could be using, is when you are commuting. If you travel by train, for example, then there is nothing wrong with using your time to read up on your latest reports or get some simpler work done. As we mentioned, this probably isn't the time for your most important work, but you might be able to knock some of the lighter work out before you even arrive at work.

If you have kids, you might find yourself having time to kill while they are awake and still need your attention regularly. This might mean taking the time to check emails while they are playing around you, or, if you have older children, you might be able to take a phone call while they are

Chapter 18: Resurrecting your dead time

in the bath (if they are old enough for it to be a safe idea). Making the most of time that would otherwise be classified as dead-time is a fantastic way to use every moment that you have to stay productive without sacrificing quality.

Keep these options in mind when you are working through your day, and try and use your dead time to make some big progress on your work and on your life. Remember, every moment of dead time that you spend effectively is another free moment to do something that you love later on! I think that makes it well and truly worth it.

Conclusion

Thank you for making it all the way to the end of this book! It has been a fantastic experience writing this and I am very thankful that you found it useful enough to read it all the way to the end!

There was quite a lot to recap in this book and I feel like I learnt a lot while I was writing it. Sure, I have lived all of these things and I've researched them for years, but there was something about putting them down on paper that has really consolidated them for me, and made the abstract so much more concrete.

By this stage of the book, you know that I am a big fan of making things concrete and actionable, and if writing down your goals, visions and deadlines into clear, specific and achievable items, so this shouldn't come as a surprise to you. Just to give you a bit of a recap for this book:

We started off with part one of this book, which focused heavily on mindset. We looked at the reason why people fail to be productive, the importance of time and where most people spend, or waste their time, as well as the power of preparation.

Part two was something that I enjoyed writing, because, as I mentioned at the start, it touched on something that I used to struggle with terribly: mastering your time. In this section, I went over a lot of things, including talking about how to plan early and well, the importance of having clear priorities and goals by adapting S.M.A.R.T goal setting, organizing your priorities and, of course, the art of setting realistic deadlines (and what a dateline is).

In the third part of this book, we had a nice, long look at the power of setting goals and how to focus on them. We started with the most important part- walking away from the negative, because unless you can break from the negative it is hard to move forward. We then went over a vital aspect of time management and goal setting, the Pareto principle, 80/20 rule, the pros and cons of multitasking, as well as the power of meditation.

Part four was another aspect that was so close to my heart, because I have battled with my energy and with letting go, for quite some time. It was

Conclusion

great to deal with increasing your energy and speeding up the tempo. On a heavier note, we also looked at determining which things are just not worth your time, speeding up the decision making process, and the benefits of using delegation, leveraging and outsourcing.

Part four was fun, and a bit of a bonus section, where we focused on how to use a to do list effectively, taking effective breaks and making the most out of your time.

Now that we have reached the end of the book, we have delved into the reasons behind your procrastination, and found your way into a more productive an energized mindset. Although this book is mostly focused on mental preparation, I am proud to say that we did have some practical tips and questions to work through.

I hope that these practical aspects have been of help to you and that you are able to use them effectively to jump start your big life change and start a more productive chapter in your life. I know that productivity can be hard, but cultivating a great mindset about it can make all of the difference and it can make or break your productivity and your results. Make sure that you always keep a good mindset, revisit your

Productivity Mindset

goals regularly and know what you are striving for.

If you can do that, I know that you will have a great deal of success. You have the talents, skills and intuition and now, you have the tools that you need for increased productivity. You are unstoppable and you need to remember that.

So good luck, keep moving forward and I wish you all of the best in your productivity journey!

www.ingramcontent.com/pod-product-compliance
Lightning Source LLC
Chambersburg PA
CBHW050233230526
45470CB00005B/1928